SO WHAT...
I CAME OUT!

"I THOUGHT I COULDN'T, BUT I DID!"

Dr. Cheryl Tilley Bost

Unless otherwise indicated, all scripture quotations are from King James Version Bible, public domain.

Published by Dr. Cheryl Tilley Bost
Douglasville, GA 30135-11156

Ordering Information: Quantity Sales. Special discounts are available on quantity purchases. Contact Dr. Cheryl Tilley Bost at (678) 933-7375 or justjesusnow@yahoo.com

Cover Design: Fivvr
Book Layout © 2022 byZeldaO, LLC

So What...I Came Out/ Dr. Cheryl Tilley Bost. -- 1st ed.
ISBN 979-8-218-03195-4

DEDICATION

To God Be The Glory for inspiring me to share my story and how I survived!

> "AND THEY OVERCAME HIM BY THE BLOOD BY THE LAMB, AND BY THE WORD OF THEIR TESTIMONY; AND THEY LOVED NOT THEIR LIVES UNTO THE DEATH."
> — REVELATION 12:11 KJV

This book is dedicated with love to my loving husband, Jaudon, who has encouraged, and motivated me to fulfill and finish this God-given assignment.

ACKNOWLEDGMENTS

With Special Thanks...

To my children, Shawn, Tara, Kika, Ziah, Yanna and Kylie for always loving, believing in me and allowing me to pour in your lives.

To my grandchildren, Tawanna Latrell, Shayna Chenique, Shawna La'Meique, Lil Shawn, Cheryl Troiauna Naymoni, Jabriyah Cheryl Tye'keriah, Kiyon, Aaron (AJ), Kyari Cheryl Faye, Kyleah Che'Fay, and Journee Denise.

To my best friend and confidant, Dr. Dadron Deon Harris, for encouraging, motivating, and pushing me to begin and complete this God-given assignment.

To the Rev. Dr. Samuel Williams, Sr., for encouraging me to continue my education even when I thought the odds were against me.

To the late Rev. Dr. Henry R. Delaney, for inspiring me to live a life that was well-pleasing to God and my spiritual mother the Rev. Ethel Y. Delaney who continuously encourages and pours into my life, as I walk this Christian journey.

To the late Willie and Eddie Mae Bonaparte-Morris, my adopted parents who loved me unconditionally, believed in me, and helped me to find my identity.

To Daisy Martin (affectionately known as Mother Daisy), your love, richness as my prayer partner, and your
commitment in typing the first phase of my man‐uscript, your kindness means the world to me.
To Selena Ryals, my longtime friend, for your editing expertise during the final phase of my book.
To Zelda Miles, for motivating, assisting, helping and encouraging me to complete my book and thank you for being my editor and chief.

CONTENTS

INTRODUCTION

DURING THE MID AND LATE 1950s,
children like myself were molested in their homes by
family members. It was so prevalent; we learned how to
deal with it. Some of us — girls and boys — just learned
to live with it, like I did. As children, we were taught and
programmed to keep our mouths shut. We couldn't talk
to anybody about the abuse. I felt my family knew,
especially my grandmother and grandfather, but they
kept quiet, too. To this day, I don't understand why.

I know there are other women who have covered up
this type of emotional trauma like I did, for over 50
years. Because of my abuse, I suffered as an innocent
child, in and out of my home; I was an emotional pris-
oner. In His love and kindness, God healed my mind,
transformed me, and transformed my life. He brought
me out, and he will bring you out as well.

I was ashamed of the abuse for years. I didn't want my
family to know, especially my children. But, when God
put it on my heart to write this book in 2019, while on
vacation with my husband in Turks and Caicos, I said,

"God, if it's going to help other women heal, I'll tell my story."

All of us have been through hurt, pain and abuse that we don't want to talk about, because we don't want anybody else to know about it. But today, as you read my story, just know that I have been delivered and I CAME OUT. Through the pages of this book, I share my story; and as you read it, I know there are still women out there who experienced, the same pain and are stuck in that place of shame. They don't want to be bothered with a man, don't know how to treat men, and have turned to women, because of the abuse suffered as a child. Some are still angry and hurt with those people who were supposed to protect them.

God gets all the glory, all the honor, and all the praise. I was able to stay strong mentally and overcome the pain, the emotion and the shame, I lived with for over 50 years. It is my purpose and decision to write this book in order to heal myself and to have an impact on others during their healing process as well.

Today, I am a happily married wife, mother, grandmother, great-grandmother, sister, auntie, pastor, and mental health counselor.

As you read my story, it is my heart-felt and sincere prayer that you will find the strength, the courage, and motivation, I did to come out of that place where hurt, shame, horror, and pain reside. If you continue to mask the pain and stay in a place of defeat, you will never come out. At the end of each chapter, you will find prayer declarations and pages to journal your emotions and help you begin your journey of coming out. You will also find at the end of the book, what I refer to as "tools for power, encouragement and strength."

— Pastor C. Bost

1 |THE EARLY YEARS

LIFE WASN'T ALWAYS EASY FOR ME as I remembered lying in bed at night crying, and hoping my mother would return for me. While she wanted to, even tried a few times, she was not allowed to take us (my siblings and I), with her. I often wondered what life would have been like if my mother raised me. To my surprise, I think my life was meant to be the way it was. A life of sexual abuse by men who were close relatives; a life that kept me suffering in silence for seven years during the abuse and over 50 years after the abuse.

Born and raised in Savannah, Georgia, the third of six children my mother gave birth to, she was a heavy drinker and drank most of the day. We lived with our grandparents in a small, raggedy two-bedroom house with a drooping front porch. I was surprised, it didn't fall down from the weight of those old couches on the front porch. My mother got married and relocated to

Atlanta, Georgia. She took my three younger siblings with her, and left the three older children, which included me, with my grandmother and grandfather.

To make sure we stayed connected and close, Grandma and Granddaddy would take us to see our mother during summer breaks and on holidays. When we got older, my grandparents would allow us to ride the Nancy Hank Train and send us to Atlanta to visit our mom and siblings. I sometimes visited more often than my other siblings because I needed to escape the abuse that no one knew about. Even though, my mother had an addiction, I was always happy to see her and spend time with my siblings. Those were some of the happiest times in my life.

During my teen years, my life took a downward turn and I began using drugs: marijuana, cocaine, angel dust, and purple haze acid. Those drugs became my comforters, relaxers, and escapers because they allowed me to escape the pain mentally. During and in my addiction, every consumption got me high, higher, and higher. In order to cover up the shame and defeat, I submerged myself in my addiction to deaden the pain, smother the hurt, and cover up the shame. I rested in that place.

My early childhood tried to define who I was and what I would become, but it didn't. Being confused and disappointed, I began to question my worth and identity. On average, I was abused four to five times a week by people I trusted, my family trusted, and yes, these were the people who abused me.

We're going to call one relative "Uncle H." Uncle H owned a service station. Oftentimes, my granddaddy would stop by and talk to Uncle H and the workers. He would hang out at the shop where they repaired tires, changed oil, and fixed cars and trucks, while I was left sitting in the truck. Whenever my granddaddy was there, Uncle H would come out and start fondling me. He would try to get me to lay down on the seat so he could penetrate me, and yes, that happened several times. He did it so quickly, I guess, he probably timed how long my granddaddy would be inside talking and cracking jokes, because he was a jokester. I would just freeze up and cry, but that didn't stop him. He would often say, "Sweetie, I love you, so you can't tell nobody about this; this is our secret." But I knew it was wrong, because I felt dirty. I knew that I had been violated because he did not do it in front of granddaddy or anyone else. It was done when he turned his back and no one was in view. Earlier, I mentioned that my granddaddy frequently visited the service station three to four times a week and every time we were there, this occurred. Every time we pulled up to his service station, my heart began to pound and beat really fast because I knew what was about to happen.

My grandmother worked two jobs; one from nine to one in the afternoon, and another from five to eleven at night, because she didn't drive. She was a maid in the homes of rich Caucasian families. My grandmother was the epitome of a Proverbs 31 woman. Although she loved us, nurtured us, and provided the best for us, I could not understand why she worked two jobs. I believe it was because our family was below the poverty level. So most of her time was spent away from home. I spent most of the time in my granddaddy's care because he worked only in the daytime; he was a gardener who did land-scaping for rich Caucasian families. When my grand-mother started working at night was when the sexual molestation escalated to every day and most nights.

The ride to my grandmother's job seemed to have been the longest ride I had ever taken. A relative or friend would have to pick her up when she got off at night. It would always be me who was told to ride with them to pick grandmother up from work; never my sis-ters, only me. So I knew, I would be fondled and molest-ed when I had to ride with him. Without fail, we always drove down Bull Street, a long, dark narrow road and four or five days a week it occurred. Whoever picked up my grandmother, pulled over on the side of that long dark road where there was not any traffic and he began to fondle me, and penetrate me. After he had finished, we went and picked up my grandmother, as if nothing had happened. Again, I had to keep quiet, I couldn't tell anybody. I had to hold back the tears when she got in the truck.

There were times, I went with my grandmother to work during the summer and that was an escape for me. My sisters and I also helped my granddaddy with landscaping at times. As a result, I have corns on my hands from raking leaves and pushing the lawn mower.

Another family member operated a service station, and we'll call him "Mr. O." The same thing happened with him when my granddaddy went to visit him. Every visit was the same for Mr. O. as well. He would fondle me maybe once or twice a week when Granddaddy went to his service station. My granddaddy would always, wherever we went, stayed in the place and left me in the truck for long periods of time.

I often wondered if it was a set up and my granddaddy knew what was happening to me. Sometimes a family friend or relative would stay the night at our house, and I would be molested in the middle of the night. My grandmother caught him one night and blacked his eyes. He was not allowed to come to our house any more. Even though she caught him, I was still afraid to tell her about the others. Much to my surprise, she didn't ask. This happened to me from age six to twelve.

Even in the midst of the abuse, and my crying, I was told over and over by the molesters, 'You can't tell anyone about this; it's our secret.' Every time the abuse occurred, they would give me a few dollars, some candy, cookies, or chips to make sure, I did not say anything to anybody about what they were doing to me.

As an innocent child, I did not tell anyone, afraid of what might happen, and because of that, I suffered so much sexual abuse. I learned how to mask the pain and cover up my emotions. During those nights and days when I suffered the abuse, I found myself lying in bed crying, and hoping someone would find out, and the abuse would stop, but it didn't.

I became sad, depressed, and fearful because I wanted to tell my grandmother, but I was afraid to tell her. Instead I kept quiet. I wanted to talk to my pastor about the abuse, but I was afraid to tell him, too. So during those early childhood years, I lived through it. I suffered through it. I cried through it, even when I kept being violated.

When I was twelve years old, I was allowed to go around the corner to Cann Park to have fun. The park was a place of comfort for me that gave me a sense of belonging, because I was hanging out with my friends. I wanted to learn how to play softball and they taught me. I was so excited because my grandmother allowed me to play softball. As a result of that, I took my hurt and frustrations out on the softball field. As soon as I got out of school, I would drop my books down and race to the park, two blocks from my house, because home was not a place of comfort and shelter for me. Home was a place of shame, abuse, hurt, and pain. It was comforting to make new friends at the park and feel welcomed by them. Being on the softball team, gave me an outlet I so desperately needed. After practicing and participating in different tournaments and leagues, I became a very good softball player. My hard work at softball led me to being named MVP. My position was pitcher and third base. I was also the clean-up batter. When I told my Grandmother, she was excited, and encouraged me to keep playing softball, so that I could interact with other children outside of church. In some ways, I thought she knew what I was going through and this was her way of helping me get some relief and find a place of safety and protection.

When I went to the park, I would stay there until dark, and then come home, do chores and homework; I would be exhausted. Some of those nights, I was awakened and molested. I struggled with homework because my grandparents couldn't help me; they couldn't read or write.

Church was a priority in our home. We were raised in the church, and I was active in various church organizations all my life. We were junior ushers and a part of the junior mission. We attended church on Sundays for worship, Tuesdays for Bible Study, Wednesdays for junior mission meetings, and Saturdays for usher board meetings. Church activities filled my childhood. When I attended church, those were some of the happiest times of my life, because it was a place of peace and comfort. After all, it was a place, I did not suffer and no abuse took place.

For me, church was both a happy place and a learning ground. At church, I learned about how much Jesus loves me and it was refreshing to sit, laugh, and play with my friends. I remembered learning and singing the song "Jesus Loves Me, This I Know because the Bible tells me so." I have so many pleasant memories about church and the things we did (me and my sisters).

The only thing that devastated me about church was how we got there. We had to ride on the back of my grandfather's truck, sitting on folding chairs. Sometimes, we would slide from side to side, but we held on to the rail of the truck to keep from falling out. We used to cover and shield our faces when we rode down West

Broad and Montgomery Streets because we were ashamed and didn't want our friends to see us. Whenever we got to church, we would hope that granddaddy would park in the back, so that our friends couldn't see us getting off the pick-up truck and tease us.

My mindset changed, as I grew older and interacted with other people; I didn't know better, I thought, all I needed to do was have sex, have babies, get married, and have a family. Nobody in my immediate family, friends, nor any relatives talked to me about the importance of an education or how life should or could be. As a result, I had to learn to cope with life the way it was and deal with every situation I faced. Most of the time, I kept quiet, especially about the sexual abuse. The more I learned from my park friends about relationships, life in general, and what a good home and family looked like, the more ashamed and violated I felt. There were times I felt unloved and worthless.

When I wasn't playing softball or at church, I was at home or visiting false friends and nasty relatives. Those are painful memories for me. I'm not sure if my light-skinned complexion had anything to do with what I experienced.

DECLARATION

Begin to speak PSALM 43:2 out of your mouth NOW. "For you are the God of my strength in whom I take refuge."

JOURNAL

Write down the emotions you are feeling at this very moment. Cry out to God and RELEASE.

DR. CHERYL TILLEY BOST

SO WHAT ... I CAME OUT!

DR. CHERYL TILLEY BOST

SO WHAT ... I CAME OUT!

DR. CHERYL TILLEY BOST

2 | ESCAPE PLAN

I BECAME PREGNANT AT THIRTEEN by my junior high school boyfriend, Al. He was my first boyfriend and my grandparents approved of him. He was a great football player, and he was very popular. I wasn't allowed to see him on weekends, but we spent a lot of time together during the week. He would walk me home from school and go back for football practice. His mother, Ms. Ann, treated me like her daughter. During my pregnancy, we spent even more time together. We both attended the same school and worked after school because we wanted to move into our own apartment. Since pregnant girls were not allowed to continue at their home-based schools, I was forced to enroll in the Model Cities Programs for Pregnant Girls. We were automatically withdrawn, and had to enroll and attend the program for pregnant girls. My boyfriend never knew I was being molested by those who were supposed to nurture and care for me, because I couldn't tell. In my thirteen-year-old mind, I started thinking, I had to get married and move out to escape my situation — not the pregnancy, but the sexual abuse.

Because my grandparents were not educated, they did not teach me the value of an education. At 14 years old, I got married to Al, he was 17, and we moved into our own apartment. During my pregnancy, I got a job at a restaurant owned by one of the church members. We'll call him, "Mr. R." I worked at the restaurant in the evenings, after I got out of school. Because of my age, I was surprised he even hired me. I really liked working there, but during down time, he began to fondle and molest me, too. It got to the point in my life, where I began to feel like this was normal. Every person who came into my life, who I hoped would protect me, molested and violated me and said, "Don't tell anybody." I heard that phrase so much, it was like it was already programmed in my mind. After six months of working there, I quit because the abuse had become an everyday thing. It didn't matter that I was pregnant, he didn't care. Trying once again to escape the hurt and run away from the pain, I became bitter and angry. I gave birth to my first child, Shawn, in March of 1973. I said to myself, "Welcome to adulthood."

In the midst of all this, I continued to attend the church, where I was raised and grew up. At a time when I needed a positive influence in my life, God strategically placed, Dr. Samuel Williams, Sr., at First Tabernacle Baptist Church. He and his wife, Claudia, had two small children, Little Sam and Mandy. I would spend time with them on Sunday afternoons, feeling loved and comfortable at their home. Being with them at their home in Cloverdale, was a place of joy, laughter and safety, because I knew I would be protected. During my pregnancy, Dr. Williams said this to me: "This is not the end of the world, Cheryl. I want you to stay in school, and when you graduate from high school, I will help you enroll in college." At Savannah State College, now Savannah State University, he was a professor and a dean; he did exactly what he promised.

I listened to his advice and did exactly what he advised me to do. I graduated from high school June 1976, and enrolled in college in September, to pursue my education, so I could have a better life and provide for us. My education, and pursuing my goals and dreams were at the forefront of my mind, every day, because I knew there was a better way and all I had to do was apply myself and stay focused. In order to do that, I realized I needed a plan; I began to save my money and live on a tight budget.

At the beginning of my college career, two things happened: my drug use increased and I gave birth to a beautiful daughter, Tara. While going to school and working a full-time job was very difficult, I was determined to succeed and be the best mother I could for my two children. After my son was born, I began experimenting with marijuana. As I suffered silently from so much pain, shame, and hurt as a result of abuse, I felt broken. Adding to the pain was my husband's infidelity. He began to have affairs after affairs; first he had an affair with my best friend's roommate, then he had an affair with my close friend's sister. The affairs continued for years, and we eventually divorced.

In spite of the pain and hurt, I was determined to work and stay in school. After enrolling in college, meeting and conversing with my professor, I knew hard work would pay off. I will refer to him as "Mr." X"; Mr. X was very intelligent, attentive, informative and convincing. He said, and I quote, "what you learn, what's in your brain, can never ever be taken away from you because knowledge is power." These words still resonate with me today. I was able to mask the pain of failure and defeat during the process.

Still hurting, I experimented with drugs during my freshman and sophomore years in college. There was a thirty-year age difference between me and Mr. X. He and I started spending time together in between classes, and we would leave campus, go smoke weed, angel dust, and periodically snort cocaine. I did not share with him either, what I experienced in my early childhood years. Even while we were getting high, he continued to motivate and encourage me. We began to get closer and closer. After a while, I began to look at his schedule, because he was a professor, and made sure my classes coincided with his so that we could spend time together during break times and between classes. He was not even aware of how strategically, I planned my schedule. Every day we spent time together at his house between classes, and I enjoyed every minute we spent together. The more time I spent with him, the more time, I wanted to be with him. Since I was abused by older men, I easily accepted love from older men, and he was the exact opposite.

We had an intimate sexual encounter after a year of spending time together and yes, it was consensual. I am now eighteen years old. Because of my age, he told me that he would not touch me until I was eighteen. Unlike before, I wasn't raped, molested, or forced to have sex. He began to teach me about sex, and how a man should treat a woman. Also, he taught me the importance of an education and to never give up on goals, dreams, and life no matter what obstacles I had to overcome. As I said, I never shared with him what I was experiencing (emotional trauma) and what I had already experienced (mental trauma). I was in love with him, because of the love and the attention he so freely gave me.

It was in his arms, I felt loved and special, so spending time with him was just what I needed. I began to track his every movement when he was away from campus and on weekends. I would ride by his house to see if he was home and sometimes, I would call and we would get together. As he would go to the places he frequented for recreation, including tennis and fishing, I would watch him do these things. He never knew I was doing this until we talked about it years later. He was very instrumental in my life and my decision making. Though, we developed a relationship first and became intimate later, he always emphasized the importance of an education and helped me achieve some of my goals.

I was reminded every day that studying and applying myself to my studies would improve my life and living conditions. Mr. X was very vital in my growth and development as a young woman during my college years. I am forever grateful to him for stepping into my life and helping me grow into the woman I am today, so that I could pursue my career goals and dreams.

As years passed — sometimes two, five, even ten or more — when I didn't hear from him, I would call around his home city to find out where he was working. He was an educator and he often taught at high schools or colleges and he would do the same to check up on me. He said to me, "You will always love me and I will always have a special place in your heart." It was easy to find him because and when I located him, I left a message with the receptionist. When he retrieved his messages, he returned my call and we talked — bringing each other up-to-date on our lives. There were those times, we would meet up and spend time together, making memories that I will forever treasure.

DECLARATION
Begin to speak PSALM 127:13 out of your mouth NOW:
"Lord, I am a heritage from you, the fruit of the womb a
reward. I'm calling on your name because the name of
the Lord is a strong tower; the righteous (child, me) runs
into it and is safe."

JOURNAL
Write down the pain that you had to endure and keep
silent about for years. RELEASE those embedded emotions today.

SO WHAT ... I CAME OUT!

SO WHAT ... I CAME OUT!

DR. CHERYL TILLEY BOST

3 | MASKING THE PAIN

I DROPPED OUT OF SCHOOL 30 hours shy of the completion of my bachelor's degree in business administration. I allowed the cares of my circumstances and drugs to become greater than my desire to finish college. Having been introduced to crack cocaine by my brother-in-law, I allowed it to control my life. I felt like school was no longer necessary because of the fast money I was making and the comfortability in my addiction. I masked my pain every time I got high. Every time, I got high, I covered up my hurt and my emotions. It didn't matter how long the abuse had taken place, those thoughts were forever plastered in my mind.

My addiction was no longer the only thing holding me captive; I was in the drug game. I met an older man who was a drug dealer and we developed a relationship. I used to traffic drugs with and for him from Georgia, Florida and to South Carolina. After picking up, testing, cutting and bagging the drugs, I distributed them to the "blade runners" (those were people who sold the drugs for us). In order to mask my pain, after all of that, I would get my drugs, go home, and get high for days. That was my routine for years. My boyfriend (the drug dealer) decided that he would have an affair with my friend, so I tried to hurt him. I hired a hitman to kill him. They shot at him, but they missed, and I am so glad they missed, because prison would have been my home. He forgave me and did not press charges (BUT GOD!).

As a result of everything that had happened to me, I was in a state of confusion. I didn't know which direction to go. Drugs were plentiful in my life, because of my involvement with my drug dealer boyfriend, as well as family members who sold drugs. Drugs eased my pain, so I thought, however they allowed me to mask the pain even the more.

At the height of my addiction, I got pregnant again and gave birth to another beautiful girl, Kika. I was now addicted to crack cocaine. I smoked crack five days out of seven days a week, as my desire for crack intensified. Some weeks, I smoked every day. I was so high when it was time to deliver her that I was able to endure the labor pains and arrived at the hospital twenty-eight minutes before she was born. At birth, she weighed only three pounds and twelve ounces.

Afraid of what medical challenges she would endure because of my addiction, I made the decision to give her up for adoption. It was my ex-mother-in-law, my previous husband's mother, who stepped up and offered to take care of her. Even though she was small, she was beautiful and healthy. I allowed my baby's grandmother to nurture and care for her and I continued in my addiction.

During the last few months of that pregnancy I met another older man, Robert, who was caring and compassionate; we developed a relationship. He was attentive and concerned about the welfare of me and my children. We were well taken care of, even though he was married. Our relationship grew stronger and stronger and we fell in love. I got pregnant from him a year later, and gave birth to another beautiful girl. He named her Ziah. She too was healthy, but premature weighing in at four pounds. In order to be close to my babies, I decided to move out on my own, but down the street from my mother-in-law so she could help me with them.

Our relationship was great and we enjoyed spending time with each other. After his wife found out about us (about a year later), our relationship had many challenges. Due to the challenges, I decided not to be in any more exclusive and permanent relationships. We talked about it on the phone, he told me that he understood and accepted my decision, but said, he wanted to take care of and be a part of his daughter's life.

Back in the day, friends and families would get together and throw house parties, play spades, sell food and alcohol to make sure we could generate extra money to pay our bills. We always supported each other.

My yard party was scheduled for that Friday night. On Tuesday, I spoke to Robert about the break-up and it wasn't until Friday that I heard from him again. I was in the backyard partying with my guests when I ran out of potato salad, and I asked him to take my son to the store to pick up more ingredients, and he did. Things were going well, money was being made, and we were playing cards and having a great time. As soon as he returned from the store, he asked me to come inside with him so we could talk. He closed the door behind us as we entered my bedroom. After closing and locking the door, he pulled a butcher's knife from behind his back and began to stab me. He had a .38 on his waist and a .45 strapped to his leg. He didn't shoot me, he stabbed me seventeen times, he apparently had been drinking earlier, as he later admitted. EMTs told me, I would have bled to death if I had drank one beer because alcohol makes blood flow more freely. I had nothing to drink that night. "BUT GOD!"

While Robert was stabbing me, I was screaming and crying out for help. In order to protect my face and chest from what could have been fatal wounds, I used my hands and arms as shields. My oldest sister, Harriet, was among the people in the yard, heard the commotion, and rushed inside and kicked my bedroom door open. I was bleeding profusely, so she panicked and ran out to get help. When my friends came back inside, he was sitting in a chair in the living room, asking our friend, Tootie to help him because he didn't know what he had just done. Several people tried to stop the bleeding while I waited for the ambulance, but I had so many stab wounds that it was impossible to stop the blood flow.

As he was stabbing me, he said, "If I can't have you, nobody else will; I'd rather kill you." I was treated and admitted to the hospital for the severe stab wounds to both my hands and my legs and had to have a blood transfusion. Because I was unable to take care of myself, I stayed in the hospital for over two weeks. Both hands and legs were bandaged up and I could not walk. I had to have around the clock care even when I was able to return home. BUT GOD KEPT ME!

Robert was arrested and charged with aggravated assault. After he was released from jail, I was told he called me several times. I was not able to answer the phone because of my hands. Whenever others, those who were caring for me, answered the phone, the person would hang up. Eventually, we found out it was him. Three of my brothers, Eddie, Gregory, and Randy came from Atlanta immediately to kill Robert, but they understood that I didn't want them to cause him any harm. They said okay, we are going to let you handle it.

Later, I received a call from my aunt informing me he had reached out to her. She told me, he apologized to her for what happened and he wanted me to hear him out. She shared with me everything he told her that led up to the stabbing and she wanted me to listen to what he had to say. Eventually, I did. He was very emotional and very apologetic, as he asked for my forgiveness. He had lost his family, his job, and he was losing me, the woman he loved, so he snapped.

I was unaware of what he was going through when I looked back on the chain of events. Since he acknowledged that he was the cause of my condition, I allowed him to come see me. He wanted to take care of me. We talked more after he visited several times. It wasn't until we talked, I understood, what triggered him to stab me. Breaking off the relationship, just fueled the fire. I had no idea he had lost his job and his family and I had become his world. I was the one person he had left and I was trying to end the relationship, and he couldn't accept it.

He asked me not to go to court because his wife wanted to see how I looked and who I was. After being subpoenaed several times, I failed to show up for court and the charges against him were dropped. Prior to the charges being dropped, I was repeatedly asked by the detective assigned to the case, if I was sure, I did not want to press charges. Repeatedly, I said, I didn't because he had never been violent with me before and had never put his hands on me. The charges against him were dismissed.

I was so in love with Robert, and despite the fact that he almost killed me, I still wanted to be with him. After he got off work, every night, he took care of me. I was bathed properly, bandages were changed, and food was provided because both my hands were bandaged.

We decided to relocate once I had healed and could move around. We knew that we wanted to be together and if we wanted to have a good life, we had to leave Savannah and move to a new city, so we could have a fresh start.

Fortunately, my mother, stepfather, and brothers understood and provided us with a place to stay until we got back on our feet; we packed up the children and moved to Atlanta, Georgia.

DR. CHERYL TILLEY BOST

The union, at his job fought for him to get his job back because he was only three years away from retirement. When the union won, the decision had to be made whether to stay in Atlanta or return to Savannah. Because I didn't want to deal with questions or conversations about what had happened between us and why I took him back, I told him we would not be able to move back to the old neighborhood.

He returned to Savannah before us to work and find a place to live. About two months later, he managed to rent and furnish a two-bedroom apartment. After visiting the apartment, which was in an upscale part of the South Side, for a weekend, I had to decide whether I wanted to come back, and yes, I did. After that visit, I returned to Atlanta, packed up the children and came back. We lived there for about two years and then he purchased a nice three-bedroom house on Greenbriar Court in the Coffee Bluff area.

DECLARATION

Begin to speak ISAIAH 41:10 out of your mouth NOW: "Lord I am still hurting and dealing with this emotional pain that I masked for so long. But I am going to fear not, for I know you are with me. I know that you are my God. You will strengthen me, help me and uphold me in your righteous right hand and I am grateful."

JOURNAL

Write down your obstacles that hindered you during your abuse. RELEASE and and write them down.

SO WHAT ... I CAME OUT!

SO WHAT ... I CAME OUT!

SO WHAT ... I CAME OUT!

4| MOTIVATED
TO ENDURE

WE GOT MARRIED AFTER his wife passed away from a terminal illness not long after we moved back to Savannah, I was still using crack, but not as much.

The only way for me to stop ignoring the pain of being molested and abused was to stop masking it. I wanted to master that pain without crack cocaine, but the devil, our enemy, was clever. When my husband got his job back, he connected with a friend who lived out in the country; this guy was making and manufacturing crack cocaine. He sold drugs for this guy, but of course, I began to smoke it. Once a month, we headed out to get pounds of crack cocaine to sell. Eventually, he felt the need to try smoking crack with me. When he smoked, the drugs made him paranoid, making him believe I was betraying him.

Even though he didn't touch me, he said things that scared me. After we talked about it, we realized that if he did not stop, we would have some serious issues. After I threatened to leave, he decided he wouldn't use any more; however, he continued to sell drugs, but he only sold to people he knew and he never sold drugs out of the house. When he was at home, I smoked a little, but when he was at work, I smoked a lot.

I once smoked crack for seven straight days without eating or drinking any water. I smoked so much, I passed out and had a seizure. There were two people in the house when I had the seizure. We had crack stacked on the dresser. The first thing I remembered after waking up from the seizure, was being covered in wet towels. Even though they kept telling me, I had passed out, I was still confused about what happened. When I began to pull myself together, I walked to the dresser and opened it, and I said, "I had a dresser full of crack, where is my dope?" They had thrown everything in the closet because they didn't know if they had to call 911, but they didn't. I looked in the closet and found all the crack right where they had thrown it. I began to smoke some more.

My husband stopped selling drugs because it was taking a toll on me and my addiction had began to spiral out of control again. Who has a seizure and starts smoking again? I could have died. BUT GOD! My body was starting to shut down, but I sat there smoking crack anyway. After we finished smoking that day, I felt like my addiction had reached another level. I wanted out, but the drugs were so plentiful, making it very hard.

The molestation and abuse left me emotionally destroyed. That's why for seven consecutive days, I thought I could mask all the pain and make it go away. It did temporarily. It was only when I wasn't high that I was able to feel the pain of the abuse. I did not want my husband or children to know what I was going through. I told myself I had to learn to manage the pain, my emotions, and my addiction. It started with getting a job.

I worked at a local hospital from eleven o'clock at night until seven in the morning. After about five years, my addiction became minimal. I still indulged but not as often. I eventually left that job and started working for Blue Cross-Blue Shield, and later Aetna. I always had well-paying, good jobs. I guess you could call me a functional addict. You wouldn't know I was addicted to crack unless you came to my house and we indulged together or unless, I bought some crack from you. When my high leveled out, I started smoking weed and drinking, then I started again. When you are addicted, like I was, you have to keep feeding the addiction with other substances, because the high only lasts for seconds or minutes.

During my time at Aetna, I had a very decent salary. But, even at my job, people were selling crack and weed (no escape). I would drive past the drug dealer's house on my way to and from work every day making access to drugs easy. I could buy and smoke crack whenever I wanted to. After spending my entire check, more than $900, in an hour and a half, it was clear I was in trouble.

When my husband asked where my paycheck was on Friday and I said it was in my desk drawer at work, he knew, I was lying and he didn't say anything. On Monday, when he drove me to work, we pulled up to the building, he said, "Go in and get your check." I walked inside knowing that my check wasn't there because I had smoked it up. The only thing I could do was go back to the car and tell the truth. I got back in the car and began to cry. "I'm sorry, I lied to you. I smoked up my entire check." His exact words were: "I knew you did and you can't continue to do this; If you do, I've got to leave. I'm not going to live with you and your addiction. You're too smart for that and I'm not going to do it. If you don't get it under control, it's going to destroy us and we're going to lose everything we have. So you have to make a decision whether you want me or you want the crack."

I loved him and wanted a better life. The decision was easy to make and I decided that day, I wanted him and not the crack. When I made that decision, I began to talk to the Lord and God gave me the strength I needed to endure.

One Sunday, we decided to visit the neighborhood church. The pastor said, "the only real peace you'll ever have will be in Christ Jesus." I allowed that to marinate in my spirit and it began to change my mindset. I was still sneaking and smoking crack, but that Sunday, those words resonated so strongly in my spirit, I made the decision to stop smoking crack. Even after I made up my mind, I still struggled with my addiction. Trying to find peace, not crack was a challenge. To avoid smoking crack, I would sometimes drink alcohol and smoke weed. Next door to us lived some Caucasian neighbors who smoked weed, drank alcohol, and used crack. So at times, I would go to their house, sit with them and we would indulge. However, the more I attended church and heard Pastor Buddy's messages, the more I wanted to be delivered. I began to lay before God and ask him to help me.

From that day on, I never looked back or started smoking crack cocaine again. I did not have to go to rehab or any treatment program. I did not relapse. I disciplined myself, so that crack would not be my desire anymore. The Lord gave me the strength to quit cold turkey and I did. I CAME OUT AND YOU CAN TOO!

DECLARATION
Begin to speak this out of your mouth NOW: "Lord, even though I walked in the midst of trouble (as an innocent child) you preserved my life. You stretched out your hands against the wrath of my enemies and your right hand is still delivering me and I am so grateful."

JOURNAL
Write down how you were able to mask the pain and cover up the hurt. RELEASE and write it down.

SO WHAT ... I CAME OUT!

DR. CHERYL TILLEY BOST

SO WHAT ... I CAME OUT!

SO WHAT ... I CAME OUT!

5| OVERCOMING THE ODDS

AT THIS TIME, I WAS working in the public school system. Some of my co-workers went to Bible study every Tuesday at one o'clock during lunch. One day, my co-worker, Anita, asked me to go to Bible study with her. Of course, the first five or six times, she asked I declined. But she didn't stop asking. Finally, one day, she came to me and said, 'I really want you to go to Bible study with me. There is enough time to go on our lunch break, and I think you'll enjoy it.' I gave in, went, and really enjoyed it.

However, I preferred eating lunch with my other friend, Pam, who was saved. She and I would eat lunch together and then she would sit outside with me while I smoked my cigarettes. One day she asked me, "Do you really love God?" I answered yes, but added that I had some challenges in my life and I'm trying to get it together. She didn't hesitate, when she added, "But do you realize that your body is a temple of the Holy Ghost and every time you smoke a cigarette you're clouding up your temple and Christ can't dwell in unclean places. So when you smoke a cigarette, your body becomes unclean."

That cut me like a knife. I decided to cut back on smoking until I was able to quit. I ignored her for a while, going out to smoke after lunch instead of meeting with her for lunch. One day, the Lord started dealing with me and my life choices. As he ministered to me through clouds of smoke, I was convicted and I knew I could fight this nicotine demon as well.

I began to go to Bible Study with my co-workers and enjoyed it. The pastor, the late Dr. Henry Delaney, using one chapter and one verse explained the scripture so thoroughly that it was easy for me to understand and retain. Following three Bible studies, I called my husband and told him I wanted him and the children to go to Bible study with me on that Tuesday evening. We went that day and the pastor prophesied to me. I'll never forget that day. I sat behind a long, white post because I was hiding and afraid, and didn't want to be called up. He said, "Young lady behind the post, come up here." I hesitated and my heart was pounding, but I went up to where he sat. He said these exact words to me, I'll never forget, "The Lord told me to tell you, He's going to protect you from your home to your job and from your job to your church, and every place else you are not going to be protected. God has protected you from a lot. His hands have been upon you for a long time. And people around you will be able to do anything they want to do, but God has placed something in you that will not allow you to do everything you want to do." After I stepped into that church for the fourth time, my life was forever changed.

I kept attending Bible study every Tuesday afternoon on my lunch breaks and on Tuesday evenings. After about a year, I decided to join the church with my children. My husband said he wasn't ready to join, but would come and support us. I talked to my pastor about this, because the enemy tried to make me feel like what I was doing was wrong. My pastor said to me, "Don't say anything to him about coming to church again. You live the life in front of him. The way you live, how you talk, how you carry yourself in your home will draw him."

I did exactly what he said and three months later, my husband started going to church with us every Sunday, attending both Bible studies, and eventually, he joined. I asked my husband to make one of the closets in our home a prayer closet for me, because I needed that intimate, private time alone with God, and he did. I began to enter my prayer closet two to three times a day, door closed, no interruptions. I knew and understood that I needed God's strength and guidance to fight against the odds. I needed God to help me fight my addictions, to overcome the hurt, the molestation, the pain, the shame, and all of the emotions I was experiencing. I pleaded with God to help me to overcome it all.

I developed a strong prayer life as a result of my pain. I would lock myself in my closet every morning at five o'clock, crying for hours, confessing my sins, and praying over and over to forgive all of the men who sexually abused me. Even though, I could not talk about it with my husband, I could talk about it with God. That closet was my place of peace and comfort. When I went into my secret place, I found the courage and the strength that I needed to get through every emotion that kept me bound.

After joining the church, I became involved in several auxiliaries and made sure that my children were as well. My pastor appointed me to be the president of an Outreach Ministry known as the Board of Evangelism. I was then asked to initiate and start a ministry for the football players at Savannah State College. We (Joyce and I) implemented a monthly feeding fellowship, ministering and encouraging the players.

Later, I was asked to start a drug ministry at the church; the drug ministry was named A.M.E.N. (Addicts Ministry Evangelistic Network). Our church had two drug programs — the Hallelujah House and the Chestina House. The Hallelujah House was for men; our pastor named it that, because he said every time someone asked the men where they lived, they would give God praise. The Chestina House was named after his mother. It was mandatory for residents from both houses to attend the meetings every Wednesday, in order to remain in the housing programs. Dedicating my time and my life to God gave me the strength to endure and sustain.

We would minister to the men and women about the importance of fighting their addiction, being delivered, living a meaningful and purposeful life. My children became very active in the church ministries, too. They were on the Praise Dance Team and they sang in the Rossie T. Hollis Children's Choir. We attended Sunday school and Sunday worship service. My entire family attended morning worship services, the three o'clock healing service and the six o'clock evening Vesper service. I became more and more involved and drew my strength from staying connected to God and ministry. GOD CAN AND HE WILL!

DECLARATION

Begin to speak PSALM 147:13 out of your mouth NOW: "Lord, I seek you for healing, strength and comfort. You know my struggle. You see my pain and hurt at this very moment. Lord, you alone can heal my broken heart. You are the one who bandages my wounds and I am so grateful."

(Begin to really pour out your heart to Him and allow Him to comfort you and HEAL those emotions and give you strength and grace to endure.)

JOURNAL

Write down where you are now in your emotions. EX-ACTLY what you are feeling. RELEASE — Let it Go! YOU have been carrying it too long!

SO WHAT ... I CAME OUT!

DR. CHERYL TILLEY BOST

DR. CHERYL TILLEY BOST

SO WHAT ... I CAME OUT!

DR. CHERYL TILLEY BOST

SO WHAT ... I CAME OUT!

6| IT WAS PAIN THAT BROUGHT PRAISE

ON CHRISTMAS DAY, DECEMBER 1995, I suffered a heartfelt loss. My husband died. He suffered from congestive heart failure. The children and I went to church that Christmas morning because we always had an hour of power. My friend, Mildred, rode with me to church. My children were now of age to drive and had their own vehicle, so they drove to and from church. On our way to church, Mildred and I sang and thanked God for allowing us to see another Christmas. When church was over, I went over to the pastor's house and we exchanged gifts, laughed, played, joked around, and had a really good time. When I pulled up in the driveway an uneasy feeling came over me; a spirit of sadness. The moment I opened the door, I could smell death, an unusual and unfamiliar smell.

Just days before, especially Christmas Eve, he had been very sick. I was in the bedroom sitting on the side of the bed praying with and for him and said, "Lord, how long will I have to watch him suffer and cannot help him?" On Christmas morning, the next day, he looked like a brand new man. His skin was so clear and smooth, no congestion and he even looked ten years younger. Before I left for church, he had asked me to prepare him a plate with a little bit of greens and rice. I did and continued to get dressed and made sure the children were dressed, so we would be on time for service. I assumed he had eaten. Then on my way out the door, I asked him if I should set the alarm. He said no, "I am going to get up." That was unusual, but I complied.

After arriving home from church, I made my way to the bedroom and I began to yell out, "Hey, honey, I'm home." I yelled as I walked down the hallway, and when I got the bedroom door, I said, "Honey, I'm back." His back was to me as I made my way into the room. I assumed he was asleep, so I stepped over to the dresser and began taking my jewelry off. Again, I said, "Baby, I'm home." He didn't respond, and as I walked around the side of the bed, to see his face, I noticed he had changed his pajamas. As I approached him, his eyes were wide open and he was just lying there. I called his name several times, shook him and he did not respond or move. He was still warm, but unresponsive. I grabbed my phone, ran to the porch, and dialed 911.

When I hung up the phone, the children were pulling up. They could tell I was distraught and crying before they reached the porch, and the asked, "Mama, what's wrong?" I said, "Your dad is dead." They lost it. He had been a good father, and provider.

The ambulance arrived fifteen minutes later, or so it seemed. I called my pastor and told him of my husband's passing. Before EMTs could get in the house, people from my church were flooding the house. The pastor had called my friend, Rosalind, and told her what had happened and to go check on us, she came immediately. I went back in the house to the bedroom and the EMTs confirmed he had passed away. Two hours passed before the funeral home arrived to remove his body because it was Christmas Day. So many people were at my house. So much love was shown that day for me and the children. People were in and out crying and trying to console them and trying to console me.

While I was sitting there in my grief, I was reminded of the Christmas morning sermon Pastor Delaney preached earlier, "It doesn't matter what happens when you get home or what you find when you get home, know that God is with us." I realized that God was preparing me for what I was going to encounter when I returned home. It was hard, and very devastating. I even got mad with God and began to question him. "God, why would you take such a wonderful man from me?"

I shared my feelings with my friend and she said to me, "Cheryl, if God gave you Robert, he can give you somebody much, much better because He is God!"

The next call was to my boss, the late Eddie Mae Bonaparte Morris, to inform her about my husband's passing. He volunteered at Saint Paul Academy for Boys and was her assistant; I was one of her secretaries in the Chatam County School System. He was there at the academy to make sure the boys stayed on task, and to do whatever was needed — errands, food shopping, etc. She must have gotten to my house in five minutes flat. She began to embrace and console me and the children. She said to me immediately, "Don't worry about coming to work, no time soon, just take as much time as you need; if you don't have the leave, I will advance it to you and whatever you and your children need, call me and I'm going to make it happen for you." There was so much love and support surrounding us. "LOVE IS WHAT LOVE DOES."

Mildred, my friend and prayer partner, who rode with me to church, had gotten her daughter to bring her back to my house soon after I had called and gave her the news. His body was still there and when she arrived, she went in the bedroom and began to pray. I knew this was going to be a very difficult time in my life. I kept thinking finally, my life was together. I was happily married and we both had been delivered and filled with the Holy Ghost living a drug-free life. Life was good, but God had a better plan. When everybody left, because of my prayer, life and my foundation, I had to go into my prayer closet. I stayed there hours, crying, praying and asking God why? God said to me, "I have always taken care of you and I'm going to continue to take care of you as long as you stay in my will."

I began to develop anxiety, worrying about how and what bills needed to be paid because he paid all the bills. I didn't know how much they were or when they were due. When I eventually looked in his top drawer, where he kept all of our important documents, I found en-velopes with checks for all our bills for the month of January, leaving me direction and guidance on how and when to pay the bills. WON'T GOD DO IT!

Every time I went in my prayer closet, I grew stronger and stronger every day. I still had a call to make. I had to call his children from his previous mar-riage to tell them that their dad passed away. That was one of the hardest things to do, but I did. It was hard because they had just accepted me as his wife and their mother had passed away two years prior. His son, the baby boy Mark, was very special and dear to my heart. He was the one who accepted me from the beginning. He let me know, he knew his dad loved me and he loved me for loving his dad.

Now, I had to deal with more obstacles; the home going service that was held on New Year's Even day. Family and friends were around for a while, but once everything was over and everyone left, the pain was still there. I began to feel broken, empty, and alone because my husband was my strong support system. About three weeks after the funeral, I was sitting on my sofa and the devil began talking to me. That demon told me things were going to get worse before they got better, and if I wanted to mask the pain and hurt, I could go buy some crack and smoke it while my children were in school and nobody would know. At that very moment, I thank God, Hallelujah, I had already had that experience and was not willing to allow myself to go down that road again. I had to mentally discipline myself. I was stronger in Christ and in my prayer life. So, I talked back to that old devil. "Devil, not this time, you won't trick me again. I've been there and the Lord has delivered me. I will not allow you to kill me, so you can try something else; but crack cocaine will not work."

I was very adamant, strong, vocal, and aggressive with the devil, because I was not going to give in. His response, "You can go and get a hotel room and just tell your children that you are going out of town for a couple of days; buy your dope, go and smoke, so you won't feel the pain and hurt you are experiencing right now." I got so angry. I yelled, "Hell no! I told you, you will never trick me again, so you can find somebody else!" I guess he did that because he did not bother me anymore about using drugs.

As my children and I worked through our grieving process, I was able to draw strength from God, my family, friends, and my church family. I kept telling the Lord, I needed help myself. I kept holding on to my faith. There were many nights I laid in bed weeping and talking to God, trying to understand why this had to happen to me. Soon, I began to rest in the arms of Jesus. I cried and I prayed. I cried and I prayed. It seemed like a dream. He was going to come back, but he didn't.

The summer came, and I finally got my children settled. The children went to spend the summer with their grandmother. That gave me time to take a couple of road trips so I could get my mind off of my pain, loneliness, and fearful emotions. I had friends who lived in Florida, so that's where I headed. While visiting with them, I laughed, had fun and really enjoyed myself.

Needless to say, that didn't work too long, because I realized I could not run away, from the pain nor my emotions. When it was time to go to sleep and return back home, those feelings, and those emotions just resurfaced all over again. They stayed with me for a long time, years and years.

DECLARATION

Begin to speak ISAIAH 61:1 out of your mouth NOW: "Lord, I feel the "Spirit of the Lord" is upon me now because the Lord has anointed me to bring good news to the afflicted. He has (NOW) sent me to bind up the brokenhearted, to proclaim liberty to captives and freedom to prisoners."

JOURNAL

Write down how your pain can help other women come out of that place of hurt and shame. RELEASE NOW and allow God to birth that ministry in you to help heal the scars that are embedded in your mind that have hindered you from releasing and healing.

SO WHAT ... I CAME OUT!

SO WHAT ... I CAME OUT!

7| GOD'S AMAZING GRACE

ALMOST A YEAR AND A HALF after my husband died, I wanted to date again. I was trying to find and fill that void in my life. I met and dated several guys, one of which I married twice. I married two more times in an attempt to find that love I was longing for, like the love that was abruptly taken away from me.

My marriages didn't last long at all because I married for the wrong reasons. I did it for companionship not love. It was then, I decided to focus more on myself, God's word, my children, and who I needed to become for them. I began to work even more in church and I stopped dating and doing a lot of things my flesh desired. For three years, my children and I did not want to celebrate Christmas at all. The memories were very painful because Christmas was my husband's favorite holiday and he would decorate the entire house and front yard, just to see us smile.

Several years later, my feelings and emotions again started to get the best of me (my flesh). In other words, I surrendered to my fleshly desires. I started looking for my old college professor, Mr. X, whom I had been involved with in the past. We connected again and began to spend time together. Soon after returning home, the pain returned. The comfort only lasted for a short period of time. Dating him wasn't the answer, and my feelings for him weren't as strong as they used to be.

In a sermon one Sunday morning, Pastor Delaney said: "There's somebody in here today that when you leave church, you're going to do wrong. The Lord told me to tell you, don't go there anymore." I knew in my spirit he was talking to me. The Word convicted me, and I went home and cried. Mr. X and I had planned to meet after church. My flesh wanted to spend the rest of Sunday afternoon with him, the hotel was already booked, but I just couldn't. He began to call, and page me again and again, but I didn't answer the page nor the phone. I didn't call him back and avoided talking to him for about a week. When I built up the courage and strength to call him, I did. He said he had been worried about me because it wasn't like me to not answer his calls nor show up.

I told him everything was fine, but I couldn't continue to see him anymore. His exact words were, "I knew this time was going to come, because I knew that you were changing and knew how much you love the Lord. I understand and I respect your decision, but if you ever need me, you know how to find me." The phone calls stopped immediately. Mind you, during that time, we didn't have cell phones, so we were not texting, we only had landlines and pagers. I respected him even more, because he cared enough about me to respect my decision and encouraged me to live the best life I could for God and my children.

I ended that relationship again, because I loved God more than those moments of pleasure. As soon as I hung up the phone from him, I felt as if a heavy burden had been lifted. God had given me the courage and strength to make a stand not to live an adulterous life any more. My spirit man was stronger because of my prayer life and the Holy Spirit, in me, would not allow me to continue in that relationship. I felt so relieved that day, and I began to grow even closer to God.

Years later, God allowed me to meet my present husband, Jaudon. We met at church. We were both saved and married. I was in the process of filing for divorce because my marriage was over. I wanted a man who loved God, had a relationship with God, and enjoyed church. Much to my surprise, he was in the same place.

Jaudon and I decided we wanted to be together, but had to follow through with our divorces. Of course, I followed through with mine first. I got divorced and made up my mind that I could not be in this relationship unless Jaudon was serious about divorcing his wife. I relocated to Atlanta, moved my parents with me so I could take care of my mother and make sure she got the best medical treatment possible. Jaudon and I talked about what we wanted, what we needed to happen in order for us to be together. He left Savannah and later divorced his wife. We decided to relocate to Atlanta, get married and live a better life. Before we got married, I sat down and told him this entire story. He was the only person all those years, I had shared this with. He made me feel comfortable enough to tell him about the abuse and pain I suffered, and the marriages that didn't work out. In my mind, if we were to continue in our relationship and marriage, communication, and honesty had to be the main ingredient. It was time to unmask my issues so I could heal. We have been happily married for almost eighteen years. God has done so many amazing things in our lives and in our marriage.

We faced a lot of obstacles and challenges. He has one biological child and, of course, that came with some drama. But God was able to bring us through every obstacle we faced. In September 2005, we got married. My brother, Edward, married us. We were blessed to work at the Atlanta Braves stadium and from that, we have been blessed beyond measure. If you do it right, God will bless it. We opened and operated a soul food restaurant that was very successful for three years until my husband was called into ministry. We just celebrated eleven years in ministry when this book was published (2022).

Besides our thriving, growing ministry, we both are mental health counselors. We are ministering, traveling, loving and enjoying life to the fullest. God has forgiven me, and God has forgiven us. — 1 John 1:9 "If we confess our sins, He is faithful and just to forgive us our sins and to cleanse us from all unrighteousness." We HAVE CONFESSED, BEEN FORGIVEN AND GOD GETS ALL THE GLORY.

DECLARATION

Begin to speak PSALM 34:1 out of your mouth NOW:
"God, I am finally FREE and I will bless you at all times
and your praise shall continually be in my mouth.

Lord, I thank you for being my refuge and my fortress,
the God in whom I trust. God I am READY to help another sister heal."

JOURNAL

Write down your method of way of surviving your
abuse. As you write it down, God is going to heal you
and strengthen you.

SO WHAT ... I CAME OUT!

SO WHAT ... I CAME OUT!

AFTERWORDS

THE BIBLE SAYS WE ALL have all sinned and fallen short of the glory of God, it does not matter what you went through, or what you have done, it is my sincere prayer that as you read my story, you will be blessed, strengthened and empowered. Yes, I was addicted to crack, SO WHAT I came out! Yes, I was sexually abused. SO WHAT I came out! Yes, I was an adulterous and promiscuous woman. SO WHAT I came out. I was stabbed seventeen times and left for dead. SO WHAT I came out. I was so addicted to crack until I began to have seizures and didn't value my life at all. I didn't want to stop. I was wrapped up, tied up, and tangled up with the devil. SO WHAT I came out!

As I exposed my pain, I covered up for 58 years, my hope is to encourage you, the reader, that God has a plan for you, in spite of the unexplainable pain you have experienced and masked for years, as I did. SO WHAT I CAME OUT AND YOU CAN TOO!

Keep the faith and trust God. There were those times in my life, I thought God had forgotten me, but I held on to the scripture I learned as a child: "For God so loved the world (me). I didn't understand it then, but I kept saying it and God saw my pain even when I thought He didn't. Life may seem difficult at times, and even right now, but God has a plan and He's going to fulfill that plan and bring purpose in your life to help somebody else.

When I look back over my life, I can say, "Look where He brought me from." I want you to know, you can come out of whatever situation you are facing. God has brought me through so many near-death experiences, for such a time as this. I have been through a lot and my story is one that hurts, but I am strong enough today and I am an overcomer. I understand today and see that God's hand was guiding me every step of the way.

I struggled with telling my story because there were times, I had to put it down and cry. Some emotions are still there, still raw, but I have begun to heal. In the writing process, I realized I had not dealt with all of the hurt. Erasing the memories out of my mind and covering up the trauma had become the norm for me. When God placed it on my heart to share my story, I didn't want to because of the pain, embarrassment and shame, but God said to me, "so many people are dealing with the same pain you suffered and dealt with, but others have not had this book to help them through their healing process."

There are so many people today stuck in a place of hurt, shame and abuse because these things were swept under the rug and never discussed. We were taught to close our mouths and not tell anybody. As a result, we had to suffer and endure. Because of the abuse, we received from those who were close to us and in our families, some women do not trust men; some men do not trust women. But let me encourage you, if you've gotten this far, you can come out! YOU CAN COME OUT!

SO WHAT, you were molested. SO WHAT, you were abused? I was too. But I came out, and you can too. SO WHAT you were addicted! COME OUT, BECAUSE GOD WANTS TO HEAL YOU EMOTIONALLY AND MENTALLY EVERY WHERE YOU HURT!

TOOLS FOR POWER, ENCOURAGEMENT AND STRENGTH

Jeremiah 29:11 — "I know the thoughts that I think toward you, says the Lord, thoughts of peace, and not of evil, to give you an expected end."

Isaiah 41:10 — "So do not fear, for I am with you; do not be dismayed, for I am your God. I will strengthen you and help you; I will uphold you with my righteous right hand. "

Prayer for Deliverance and Strength
Father in the name of JESUS, I stand on faith and the power and authority I have as a believer in Jesus Christ. I know that you are the only answer and you are my deliver, strength, strong tower and protector. Thank you Lord for when the enemy comes up against me, the spirit of the Lord with raise up a standard against him. Condition my heart that I may forgive those who hurt

and abuse me and I will forever give you praise, honor and glory. Lord, I know you will keep me in perfect peace, if I keep my mind stayed on you because I trust in you.

Affirmation for Strength to come out of your pain
I declare that God's favor is on me, that He has given me His Strength, Wisdom, Blessings and Peace every day of my life. I shall come out, I will come out in Jesus Name! I will not live in bondage and shame any longer. SO WHAT I CAME OUT!

I THOUGHT I COULDN'T, BUT I DID

By Dr. Cheryl Tilley Bost

I thought I couldn't quit
I thought I couldn't stop
I thought I couldn't do it
I thought I wasn't good enough
I thought I wasn't special
I thought I would never survive
I thought I would never succeed
I thought I would never make it
I thought I would never finish it
I thought I would never come back
I thought I would have to live in my label,
in my hurt, in my situation
But, I came out of it all by the grace of God
I came out of incest
I came out of adultery

I came out of homelessness
I came out of sex addiction
I came out of drug addiction
I came out of single parenting
I came out of scandals
I came out of church hurt
I came out of alcohol
I came out of abuse
I came out of not being loved by my family
I came out of not being accepted
I came out of a mental breakdown
I came out of depression
I came out of backbiting
I came out of hopelessness
I came out of disappointments
I came out of hurt
I came out of shame
I came out of pain
I came out of low self-esteem
I came out of lack of confidence
I came out of mental instability
I came out of being stabbed 17 times
So what I came out and so can you.
"I CAME OUT AND SO CAN YOU!"

ABOUT THE AUTHOR

Cheryl's story begins with the wonderful amazing power of God's grace and deliverance. Having been addicted to crack cocaine for over 15 years, suffered abuse, she knows the struggle. God birthed this vision "SO WHAT.. I CAME OUT" to encourage others that they too can come out and be free.

After coming out of her place of hurt, pain, sexual abuse and addiction, she accepted the call on her life in August 1998.

She is the CEO of Savannah Safehaven Center, Inc., and Unified Service Consulting, Inc., ministries that help to

restore, spiritually prepare, equip and empower women. She
also serves as a lead adjunct professor and the admissions
director at Kairos Voices Spiritual School, equipping and
mentoring students. She presents lectures and creates
supplemental instructional materials.

She has a deep compassion for women who have
experienced addiction, molestation and abuse by facilitating
workshops, conferences, and speaking/preaching
engagements. Her mission is that everyone who has
experienced abuse knows that "they can come out." "SO
WHAT... I CAME OUT! is a movement for women who are
struggling with addictions. Cheryl has also birthed and
currently hosts a weekly Women Only Teleconference call -
W.W.I.A. (Women Walking in Authority) every Tuesday
night at 8:30pm (1-563-999-1532) to minister to women across
the globe who are trying, have tried and want to come out of
their place of addiction and pain.

Cheryl was a featured guest on two local TV shows, "Gospel
Talk Live and TBN." Currently, she teaches substance abuse,
sexual abuse and anger management classes to help women
move from that place of pain and abuse. She, too,
understands what it is like to see beyond what others might
have predicted for you. Cheryl serves as a guiding light, as
she lives and encourages others with her favorite scripture: II
Chronicles 7:14: "If My people, which are called by My name,
shall humble themselves, and pray, and seek My face, and
turn from their wicked ways, then will I hear from heaven,
and will forgive their sin, and will heal their land."

Made in the USA
Columbia, SC
05 June 2023

17667681R00065